Popeye, Unchained

M. G. Stephens

collages
Archie Rand

SPUYTEN DUYVIL
New York City

Some of these poems have appeared in the following magazines:

Jerry Jazz Musician, Gargoyle, Gabriel's Horn (UK), The Quiver Review, Mikrokosmos Journal, Rat's Ass Review, The Last Leaves, Oddball Magazine, and *Solstice.*

Special thanks to photographer Keith Marlowe for his careful edit of the collage scans.

Minute at first, the thunder
Soon filled the apartment. It was domestic thunder,
The color of spinach. Popeye chuckled and scratched
His balls: it sure was pleasant to spend a day in the country.

—John Ashbery

Parsimony, like
Wimpy, promises to pay
You Tuesday for a

Hamburger today, Olive
Oyl slinks off with Bluto, just
To piss off Popeye

CONTENTS

POPEYE ONE SUNDAY IN THE PARK

"I am what I am, Olives, and that is
All I am," Popeye told his partner as
They walked along with their dear, sweet, Swee'Pea
In tow. It was New York or Paris or
Chicago, no palms or palmettos, just
Elms and oaks and juniper trees about
The urban park in which they walked, early
Sunday morning, sunny, no clouds skyward.
Then a gang of youths surrounded Popeye
And Olive and Swee'Pea, threatening them
With a world of hurt, "getting Medieval,"
One of these jokers said to Sir Popeye,
So he cracked open a can of spinach,
And kicked their bony, sorry asses good.

SPRING CHERRY BLOSSOMS FALLING

I was sleazy and homeless but I had
A book contract and a ton of words in
My head, waiting to be unleashed in spring
Air, walking near the reservoir, cherry
Blossoms blooming everywhere, people
Sauntering in the park; I was with someone,
A girlfriend, though that day we were breaking
Up or at least discussing the idea.

They came out of nowhere, a gang of teens
Wielding knives and boxcutters, threatening
To kill us if we didn't have money
For them. I didn't, but she did, handing
It over to the violent young thugs,
Who ran off in falling cherry blossoms.

J. WELLINGTON WIMPY

He sniffs the air and contemplates the three
Syllables in the word "hamburger," and
Thinks how glad he would be eating one of
Them under a flamboyant tree in mid-
Afternoon, the treat garnished with onions,
Pickles, ketchup, mustard, and relish, with
A side order of sweet potato fries.
But, alas, alack and goddamn, he's broke,
And it is as if he was poor a long
Time ago, but still remains broke right now,
Penury and inanition, not to
Mention downright skint from perpetual
Indigence and urban maladies of
The long-time unemployed seems to stalk him.

CLIFF-HANGER

Olive Oyl hung from a ledge by fingers
Slowly cramping and going numb, as well
As Bluto tickling her foot with agile,
Deft fingers. The erotics of the mo-
Ment drove a wedge up through her tingling bod
That made her Bluto's for that one moment,
Just before Popeye showed up jacked on cans
Of spinach turning the lad into a
Psycho lunatic. She sent him packing
That night and brought Bluto back to her place,
Where he undressed her, but she would not do
The beast with two backs or missionary
Position until he drove her crazy
Tickling her feet until she cried, *Uncle*!

SOME KIND OF LOVE POEM

From this position, love appears, or from
That angle, there it is, though completely

Unexpected, even a surprise, and
Maybe not even welcome, after all,

There are so many other things to do,
Like going to the gym or making lists

Of things to do, love not being one of
Those items listed, and yet love is there,

Unexpectedly or not, love wants you
To know that it is all that you need or

Ever wanted, even when you ask it:
Is that all that love is? And the answer,

Of course, is, yes, that is all that love is,
That is all love will ever be, and more.

ALBA FOR THE NEW YEAR

Who you are and how you got here are one
And the same dilemma. That you are here

Is a certainty. What you plan to do,
I have no idea, and I'm not asking,

So the uncertainty is another
Part of the equation. The past is past,

And that is certain, but the future is
Nothing but uncertainty, a mere dream

A conjecture. I don't know when you leave,
Or where you will go, that is another

Variable. So here you are, and here
I am, and since it is almost the dawn,

I hear birds singing in the branches of
Trees outside the window, light coming up.

ACCORDION TO POPEYE

Popeye played his favorite instrument,
Melodious boyhood accordion,
A machine, he said, was according to
The Sailor Man (*toot, toot*), the measurement,
The scale on which such heavenly music
Was weighed, like the way a butcher had weighed
Meat upon scales, not of fate but justice,
And how he, in turn, was finally paid.
But Olive Oyl stood off in a corner,
Dressed in black, veiled, like a widowed mourner,
Wondering when (*toot, toot*), this Sailor Man
Was going to put down that infernal
Accordion and come up with a plan,
According to Olive, now speaking plain.

SWEE'PEA SPEAKS

My name is Swee'Pea, and I am over
One-hundred years old, though I still slither
Across the rugs on the floor like I was
A slug or a snail, a malformed child of
God if not Popeye and Olive, I am
Their baby, more or less, by adoption
Or subterfuge, they are now my parents,
Like it or not, I am theirs, and they're mine,
The courts agreeing to award them me,
Swee'Pea, aging Infant of Prague, old man
In diapers. But when no one is looking,
I like to smoke large Cuban cigars and
Gamble on the ponies or play numbers
With local bagman, my good friend, Wimpy.

BLUES IN C MINOR

Wimpy sat in a funk because it was
Tuesday and he had no dough for those folks
He owed outright or needed to pay the
Vig, the interest on his non-bank loans
That he had transacted with the loan sharks
On Broadway, this highway to Hell he walked
Up and down upon, looking in gutters
And back alleys for the answer, prayers
Finally the only solution for
His chaotic, under-employed ran-
Dom life lived at the edge in flophouses
And juke joints, listening to the Modern
Jazz Quartet, his heart beating out rhythms
From Percy Heath and Connie Kay, et al.

JAZZ

Half-crazy and broke, I walk in the rain,
An adrift fifteen year old runaway,
Whose world is a wet paper cup of pain
And extreme hunger, teeth aching, clothes soaked,
Hair unfurled down my shoulders as I trudge
Through Cooper Square on my way to St. Marks
Place, bones on fire with fatigue, shivering
In a beat-up old coat, paper in shoes,

I haven't bathed in at least a week or
Changed my underwear even longer, but
My life is about to change as I step
Into a small club where Thelonious
Monk is performing a set, I sit at
The bar mesmerized by his jazz rhythms.

EPISTROPHY

There is music in my head, Popeye thought,
And it is the improvisational
Piano music of Thelonious
Sphere Monk, spontaneous, urban, and real,
The music of my mind, Popeye decid-
Ed, as Monk played "Epistrophy," what he
Usually played just before the band took
A break, a kind of signature bit of
Jazz, Monk playing something completely not
The same as his band, but that is exact-
Ly what Popeye liked about listening
To Thelonious Monk, improvising
Wildly on the keyboard, and then winding
Up where his group was on the last blue note.

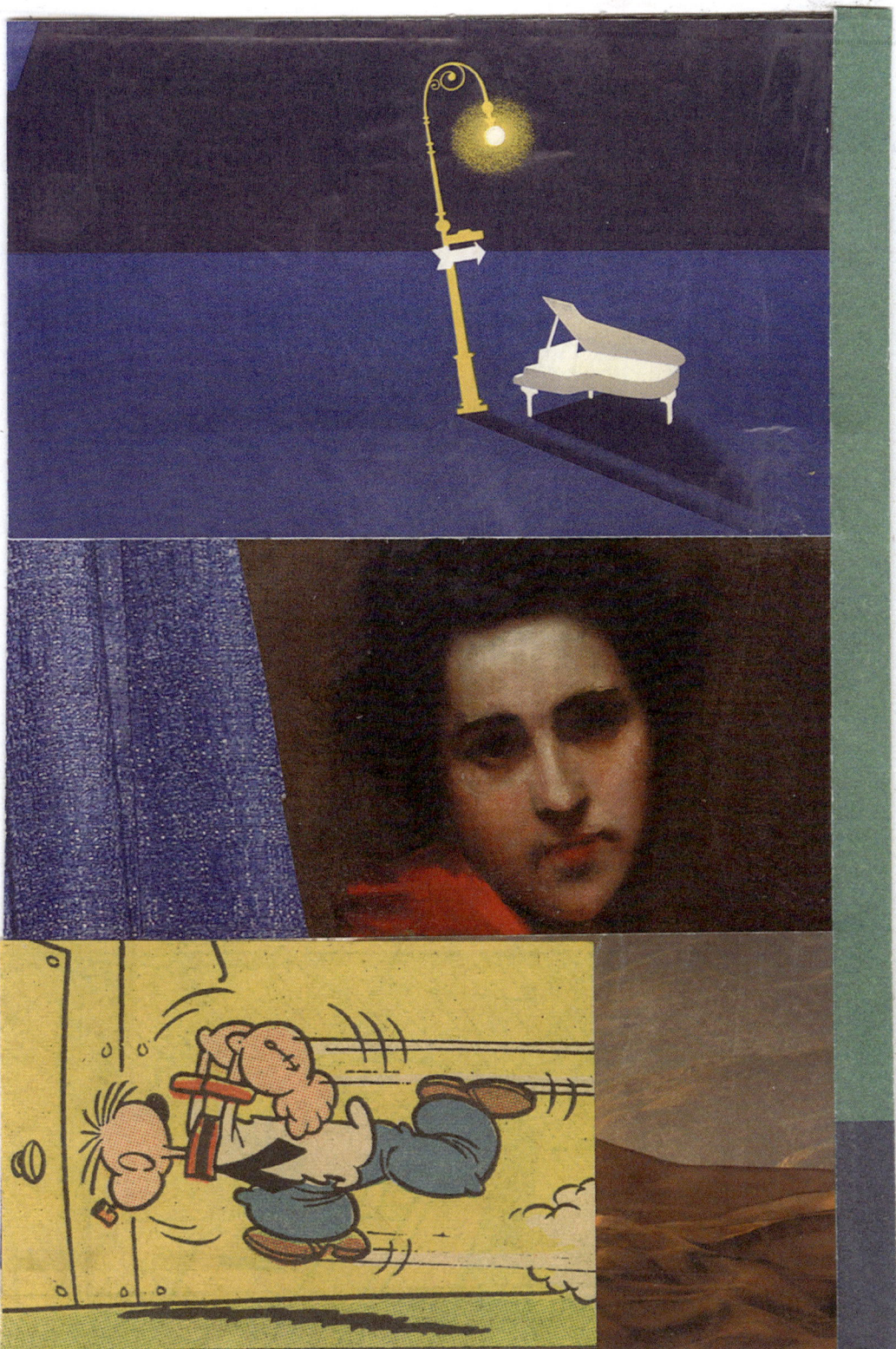

COLTRANE ON THE BOWERY

It wasn't here but over there across
The street and down the road a bit along

The Bowery, the bums drifting along
With their alcohol hallucinations,

While Monk and Coltrane were inside the Five
Spot Café, the pianist and the sax

Player up there having a musical
Dialogue, deep as anything Plato

Or Socrates laid down in Dialogues
A few thousand years ago in Athens.

Monk and Trane made history up there on
That improvised stage, improvising life

And their music, spontaneous, alive
And in the moment, ineffable, real.

AT THE FIVE SPOT CAFÉ

Visions of Thelonious Sphere Monk at
The club piano, playing "Monk's Dream"

Or "Green Chimneys" or "Well You Needn't,"
Man oh man, those were great nights to be there

When the musical genius in the fedora
Showed up four hours after he was due to play,

But none of the customers seemed to mind
The wait for his appearance outside on

St. Marks Place (there is no apostrophe
In the name, motherfucker), the Countess

On his arm, and her Silver Cloud Rolls-Royce
Illegally parked outside, he bops in,

The room hushed with this jazz apparition,
One in the morning, but things just starting.

POPEYE RUNS OUT OF SPINACH

Popeye went to London and got fitted
For a bespoke suit from a men's shop, not
On Savile Row, which he personally
Did not care for, but to Jermyn Street where
He felt right at home with shoes on sale for
Five hundred pounds, but whenever he was
In port, not in London, but near enough
In Southampton, he trained to Old Blighty
For fish and chips in Covent Garden, then
Tootled over to Jermyn Street for some
Male clothing porn, a pair of brogues, some breeks,
A fetishy green tweed cape he would say
Was for Olive, but in his size, so she'd
Thank him for the thought, but let him keep it.

BLUTO'S CANON

Bluto lambasts Popeye for his poor taste
In literature. "Take T. S. Eliot,"
The Big Galoot says to the strong sailor.
"I prefer his literary essays
And his *Four Quartets* to anything in
The Literary Canon." Popeye smiles
And giggles, not sure what Bluto talks of.
Popeye wonders: "Does the brutish Bluto
Say this just to impress lovely Olive
Oyl?" She sits on a park bench reading her
Favorite author Joyce Carol Oates, who
Has written "a gazillion books," Mizz Oyl
Tells Bluto one afternoon when Popeye
Is fishing with Swee'Pea and friend Wimpy.

COVID-19

It didn't care about who you were or
Where you had been or how you were going

To get there. It was in no hurry to
Get where it was going as long as it

Got there all right, unsafely lodged in lungs
And other tissue of the body, no

Problem waiting, it could wait for the end
Or it could make you as sick as they come

Without any problem on its part, and
It didn't care if the stakes were high, life

And death, that's what it lived to do to us,
Take us from life towards death, singing to

Us as it squeezed the breath out of each one
Of us, one by one or in groups that once

We all gathered in before the virus
Decided that it would lay each one low.

SAIL ON, SILVER MOON

This malefacting somnambulist keeps
Impregnating my mind with his goofy
Shenanigans, which is just his way to
Distract me from me primary porpoise,
Which is another way of saying he
Stinks, the dirty degenerate bully
And bunco artist, a side-show from my
Darling Olives, the queen of the May and
Soulmate of me enlarged liver and heart,
Fairy godmother to Swee'Pea, whose real
Momma was a crack whore working the streets
Around the piers from which I sailed in the
National Maritime Union wherein
I paid dues but endured no benefits.

THE FLIGHT DECK

They put him on the hospital flight deck,
Where he sat around playing Coleman Hawkins

Records on the cheap record player some
One or other found for him, so he had

At least some music to listen to as
They dreamed up some clinical diagnosis

To explain how a musical genius
Found himself stranded at a traffic light

In midtown Manhattan during lunch hour,
And him unable to unfreeze himself

From the steering wheel as the cop tried to
Pry his fingers off the wheel, put him in

The red ambulance and sped off uptown
To the immaculate hospital ward.

BLUTO'S ORBIT

From QAnon to *qi gong*, the papers
Filled Bluto with their observations, night
And day, Fox News, *National Review*,
X (the former Twitter), Elon Musk, and
Donald Trump himself, telling Bluto of
Stolen elections, Dominion voting
Machines turning everything to Joe
Biden. "But at least President Trump put
Three good judges onto the Supreme Court,
And we got rid of that godless Roe v
Wade, abortions became illegal once
Again," though he was for Olive ending
An unwanted pregnancy that started
In Texas and ended in Chicago.

SPRING DESIRE

Olive slipped Wimpy something to think of.
"What is it, Precious Desire and Love-Slave?"
"Me undies, you lout," Olive Oyl told him.
"Me thinks you mistake me for himself,
Mister Mysterioso, Popeye the
Sailor Man," said J. Wellington. *Toot, toot,*
Said Mizz Oyl, who wore a simple black dress,
Reminding him of one Audrey Hepburn,
Fashionable and understated, she—
She brought to mind Jackie O's elegance,
Especially Mizz Oyl's dark sunglasses.
If she wasn't with Swee'Pea, Wimpy would
Have trundled her off to a hotel near
Washington Square Park in Greenwich Village.

HOLLYWOOD

The moon appears over the top of a
High-rise building on Sunset Boulevard

In West Hollywood just before sunrise
On a late September morning, almost

As if it were an ingénue giving
A great performance; it is a harvest

Moon, glowing and confident, autumnal
In a way that makes life seem beautiful,

Which it isn't always, and if you don't
Believe me, ask those people under the

Overpass, living in a tent: father,
Mother, and four children, the parents working

Two jobs each, the children falling behind
In their respective grades at the local school.

RECOVERY

Popeye was peckish, Wimpy just hungry,
But then again he always was starving,
Swee'Pea was sucking on a bottle of
Fresh milk from a nearby cow, Guernsey,
Olive said, and then noted that she was
Anorexic most of her life until
She attended a 12-Step program for
People with eating disorders, people
Like herself, eating and purging, eating
And puking, binge and evacuating,
Going back to when she was an orphan,
Living in a home on Staten Island,
Meeting Dorothy Day on the ferry,
Dot got Ol to become more spiritual.

UNTIL

Bluto looked at the sky, nearly in tears
Over how beautiful the blueness was,
And how it affected Bluto's dark moods,
So he went down to the lake to observe
The gulls and finches and the aggressive
Red-wing blackbirds, some of whom dive-bombed him
Until he swatted them away, but he
Did not escape the red wings until he
Ran away from their nesting area,
So he did not relax until he was
Far from the blackbird nests, and then relaxed,
He sat on the ground after spreading a
Picnic blanket and unpacked a hamper
Of bread and cheese and water and some fruit.

RED-WING BLACKBIRD

As he walks past their nest,
A male red-wing blackbird
Dives at him, pecking away at
His head and then his hand

Which tries to swat it away.
Crazy bird, cease and desist!
Oh, brother, he wants to shout,
We are both pugilists, only

I am retired and you are more
Determined than ever to make
A case for fisticuffs and this

Reckless, suicidal dive-bombing
That mindlessly overtakes you
Red-wings every spring by the lake.

SWEAT-WICKING UNDERWEAR

Popeye is pissed about something or some
One or some other concern that drives him
Into a twist, including the twist of
His knickers, a set of Ibex undies,
Pants and T-shirt made of wool, wicking sweat
From his body, but clearly not making
Him any calmer, less agitated
Than he had been on waking that morning.
Of course, Bluto is never far from his
Spinach-fueled ire, and Popeye's ire is on
Fire, burning a hole through his new fancy
Wool underwear, and Popeye swears Bluto
Is the one who borrowed his gas-powered
Chainsaw to chop down the nearby palm trees.

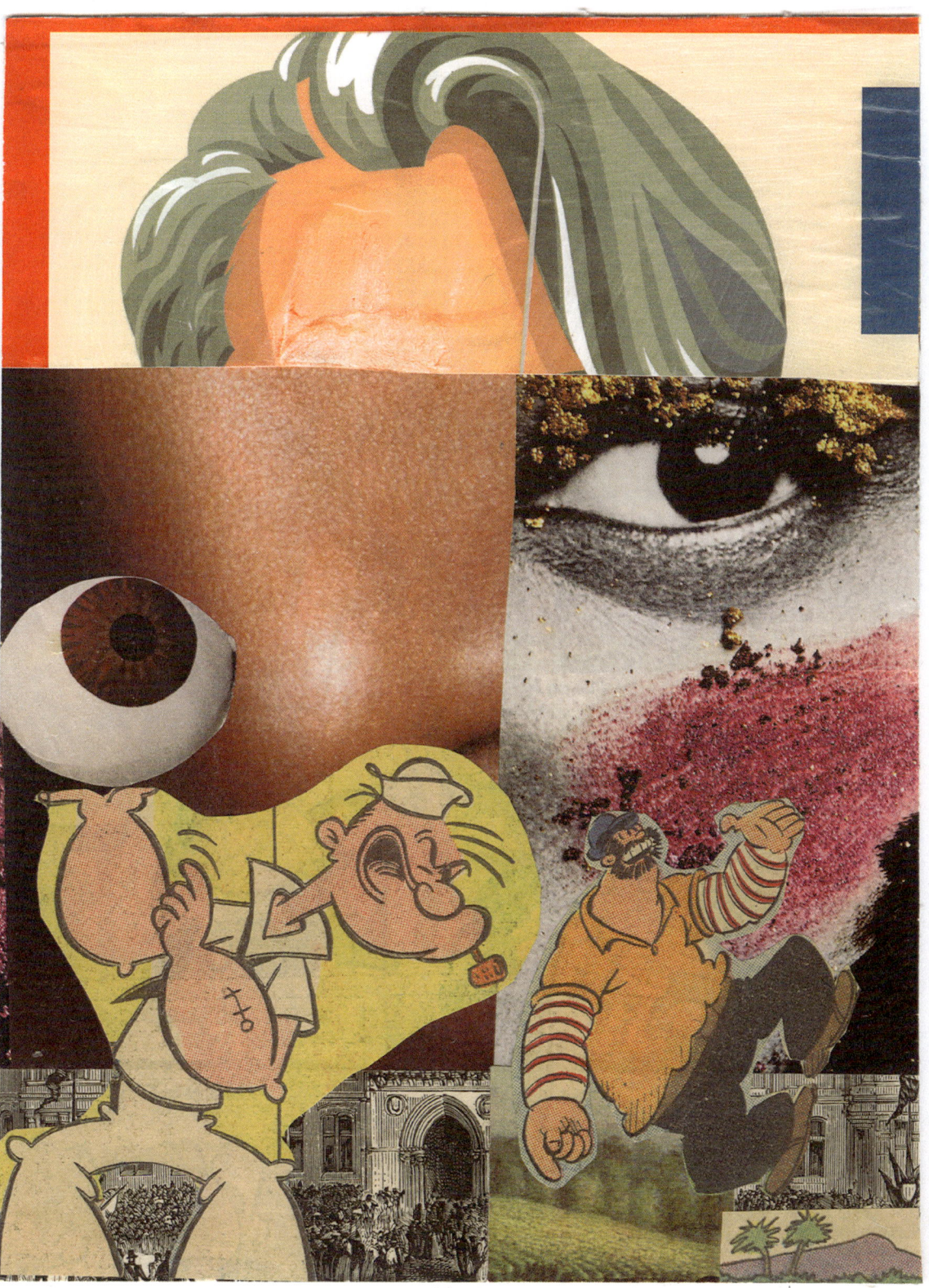

FEMININE MYSTIQUE

"I'm any man's woman," Olive
Said, "if they tickle my feet
A certain way at a certain time
And on a certain day," Mizz Oyl
Continued. "It has nothing to do
With loyalty or my being
Faithful. It's biology," said Olive.
"It's my feminine nature I guess,
It's how I am constellated."
Popeye faux laughed, opened a can
Of spinach and stared mournfully
At its green contents, its place in
His evanescent life, chuckled
And went off to work down the piers.

WIMPY INVEIGHS AGAINST INEQUITY, PENURY & INANITION

"I want your attention," Wimpy shouted.
"I'm exhausted from lack of nourishment—
My inanition, my lack of food, my
Hunger makes me insane with anger, and
I see you all going to McDonald's
For round after round of hamburgers and
Side-orders of perfectly execut-
Ed fries with giant Slurpees or huge Cokes.
How could you do this to J. Wellington,
My pets, semaphores, and onion eaters,
While your affluence is an affront to
My extreme poverty, just as my des-
Titution is an affront to your sense
Of order in the suburbs of the world.
My poverty is compounded by your
Affluence, just as your abundance is
An affront to my indigence, a state
Of extreme poverty, my penury,
My destitution, which makes you laugh at
Me because I am a figure of fun.
But I really would pay you Tuesday for
A hamburger today. Even a veg-
Etable patty made of soy beans and
Sawdust from a pulverized wooden horse."

IN MEMORY OF GEORGE FLOYD

How does one person kill another? Ask
George Floyd? He could tell you if he was still

Here, but he's not. He's gone; they took the breath
From him, then they took the life out of him.

It's as simple—or complex—as breathing
Or not breathing, and George told the police:

"I can't breathe!" How does a policeman do
That, kill a human being? Tie him up

In handcuffs behind his back, then shove him
Down on the ground, and put your knee into

His neck at the carotid artery:
Hold for at least eight minutes. Floyd called out

For help, but the police blocked anyone
From trying to help him to stay alive.

KAZAKHSTAN

The apple in the palm of my hand is
Nothing like the apples in my crazy

Head, going back to the bitter tastes of
Childhood, the apple vinegar of pain

And the rotten apples of old angers
Going back to the root of every-

Thing, the abuse in Brooklyn, in the house
And outside the house on the street, apples

In a paper bag, bought from a horse-drawn
Cart, these vivid memories are as if

Nothing compared to the apples of rage,
The apples of never-again, of no

Forgiveness, apples of merciless tears,
The torn curtain flapping out the window.

THE DAY YOU DIE

"The day you die," Popeye said, "is like all
The others—only it is not like those
Others at all, it is less than twenty-
Four hours." Olive wondered what kind of nut-
Job she had hooked up with this time, men not
Being what she was best at, men weren't
Her gift or her super-power, Swee'Pea
Was what she cared about, the little guy
Was who she lived for, him and poetry
And flowers, good friends and her family,
However broadly she defined this word
Family: Swee'Pea, Popeye, Bluto, and
All the others, the Sea Hag, for instance,
And Olive's former boyfriends and lovers.

POPEYE FREE

The world goes to Hell in an express train
From Boston to Washington, D.C., yet
I am Popeye the Sailor Man, *toot, toot.*
I still have energy and excitement
For people and things all around all of
Us, it excites me in ways I never
Imagined possible. Take Olive Oyl,
The love of my life, almost my wife, but
Not quite, we be too intimate for just
Husband and wife, and she makes me fuller,
More rounded, I can look at Bluto or
Wimpy or Swee'Pea with more love in heart,
Less fear in how I walk down the New York
Streets, open, loving, naked, willing—free.

LONDON RULES

Mizz Olive Oyl was sat in her parlour
Reading Emily Dickinson, poet
That Olive felt was one of the greatest,
Though she also dipped into poetry
By Wanda Coleman, June Jordan, and Beat
Poets Allen Ginsberg, Jack Kerouac,
Anne Waldman and Diane di Prima. Ann
Sexton, Robert Lowell, Sylvia Plath—
Poets Mary Oliver and Louise
Gluck, Sharon Olds, that Polish poet who
Won the Nobel Prize for Literature,
Ah, yes, Symborska, always a treat on
Chilly, overcast days that reminded
Her of that long exile spent in London.

BLUTO'S MAGA HAT

Bluto argued with Olive about the
Upcoming primary in which they were
At odds. Bluto wore a MAGA red hat,
Wearing his heart, not on his sleeve, but head.
Olive said, "I'm a yellow-dog Demo-
Crat. I'd rather be boiled in oil than vote
For Trump." Bluto called her a never Trump,
A Trump hater, and probably a far
Out, out of touch, left-wing Communist
Or if not, then definitely a way
Out Socialist who wants to destroy our
Country. Olive laughed her laugh, and she said:
"What you mean is you want to get rid of
Medicare and Social Security."

PRAISING DARNELLA FRAZIER

Darnella Frazier went out to go to
The store. Seventeen years old, already

She had a sense of justice and being
On the right side of the story, she stopped

In her tracks and recorded on her phone
What was happening with the police and

The poor Black man with a knee in his neck,
Cutting off the blood supply to his brain.

His name was George Floyd, the man who made us
Aware that Black lives do matter, not just

A slogan to someone like Darnella
Frazier who later when asked why she taped

George Floyd's death, she said that the world needed
To see exactly what happened to him.

SWEETPEA (SIC)

"When I grow up," Swee'Pea said, "I want to
Be just like Pernell Whitaker, a great
Lightweight boxing champion, fisticuffs
A sport I believe I could certainly
Excel at, being raised by Popeye the
Sailor Man, *toot, toot*," the tike exploded.
His father or stepfather or surro-
Gate parent let out his signature laugh,
Which also was weird and gnomic, chuckle
That it was, more a nervous tick than real
Character trait or even a guy's flaw,
A kind of Achilles heel that would side-
Line the sailor, sooner or later, if
He didn't wise up and see a good shrink.

DIOSCURI

Benny Leonard went to town riding in
A yellow cab up into Harlem to
See his mother and the rest of his kin
On Pleasant Avenue, there to assure

Mother he would not disappoint her or
The family, and that he would enroll
At the City College of New York on
The other side of town just off Broadway

And West One-hundred-and-thirty-seventh,
To study in the pre-med program, and
So to become a doctor of medicine.

But instead Benny went to the fight gym,
And became, some said, the greatest lightweight
Champion to lace on the boxing gloves.

THIMBLE THEATRE

"You're a typical pugilistic kind
Of Irishman," Bluto said to Popeye
After they boxed several one-minute
Rounds in the Sailor Man's (*toot, toot*) basement,
Where Popeye had set up a ring, punching
Bag, heavy bag, jump ropes, and many 12
And 16-ounce leather boxing gloves, which
Made Popeye chuckle. "I is Polish, born
There and come to America as a
Tike, growing up in various slum-sized
Tenements, a sickly skinny weakling
Child until me mam fed me green spinach
From tin cans, I grew up with *muskills*, and
New determination to fight all wrongs."

HAPPY, HAPPY

J. Wellington Wimpy, removed his lid,
A homburg-like sombrero, and bowing
His head, he stood silent for a minute.
It was January 15th, Martin
Luther King Day, a Monday, but also
Really King's birthday. The reason Wimpy
Knew this fact was because it also was
His own mother Rose's birthday, so he
Removed his hat and bowed his head because
That simple woman who bore him taught him
Everything he knew about being
Kind he learned at her side, standing in her
Kitchen as she baked an apple pie for
His own birthday, which was Monday, March 4th,
A leap year which explains this extra line.

ARS LONGA

Bluto had a photo taped to the wall
Above his desk where his iPad was sat.
It was a photo of Snoop Dogg and his
Good friend Martha Stewart. The caption read:
"One of these people is a convicted
Felon." In a photo of Popeye and
Bluto, he wondered, which one of them would
People pick as the convicted felon,
And why? I'm the one who buys flowers for
Olive; I am the one who weeps over
Sentimental Willie Nelson country
Songs. I am the one, yes, I am the one,
Who reads and writes poetry for Olive.

KENT STATE

I had all the time in the world until
I did not have any time at all, rush

Here, rush there, and just the other day, out
For a walk then home to read newspapers

Online, I realize it's May 4th again,
And I remember that haunted photo

At Kent State, the dead man shot down by our
Own soldiers like they do in banana

Republics the world over, and I think
Once again about that young woman, her

Name Mary Ann Vecchio, a fourteen-
Year-old runaway, caught in mid-scream, the

Fallen Jeffrey Miller at her feet, and
Mary Ann now sixty-four-years of age.

VENICE GLOAMING

Popeye won the Publisher's Wearhouse prize,
Not the one for millions of dollars, but
For a free trip of a week in Venice.
The Sea Hag watched Swee'Pea, while Popeye and
Olive flew to Marco Polo Airport,
Where they rode a bus to Mestre, a few
Miles from Venice; they would take a tram to
The Grand Canal. They walked at dusk amid
A fog creeping in on catlike feet, moon
Coming up over the lagoon, Olive took
His hand in hers, they stopped among shadows
And the night slipping in, embraced, kissed
And declared their love to one another.
He said: "I loves ya." She said: "Oh, Popeye."

MEDITATION ON VENICE

In this light, at this time of day, Venice
Is nothing but a long, slow mood, music

To fill the lacuna between Po and
Piave, its world perched on a precipice

On the Lagoon between the real and the
Imagined, reality and a pleasant dream.

Olive told Popeye there are four-hundred
Bridges to help remember and forget.

Old lovers go out for their post-prandial
Walk, only to return home to watch the

Evening news on tv to find themselves
Rendered into young lovers, and its re-

Verse, the young out for the passeggiata
Come back home transformed into old people.

WHO KNOWS WHERE THE TIME GOES

Olive dilates on her predicament,
Depredations of the environment,
And also sky-rocketing inflation,
Not to mention the wars everywhere,
Homeless children in Gaza made orphans
By the expanding Middle East conflicts,
The simple fact that Black Lives Matter, yet
America has its collective head
Up its own ass. "What is to be done, I
Ask you, Popeye the Sailor Man?" *Toot, toot,*
He yodels back at his fly old lady.
"What is to be done?" he asks rhetorically.
"Yes, what is to be done?" Olive inquires.
He scratches his balls and says, "I don't know."

ORPHEUS IN LESBOS

Orpheus came to Lesbos and he found
The carnage of immigrants, their death camps

Set up improvisationally by
Once wine-dark sea, no hope in their faces,

Even when they brought forth their progeny,
Or especially when the women slipped

Into labor and their moanings were heard
Through the miserable night of their statelessness.

Meanwhile the tour boats never abated,
Their clients avid to snap photographs

That contrasted the sheer elegant grace
Of the cloudless azure skies, salt water

Churning up metallic gray and somber
Waves, cresting with immigrants in small boats.

THE WRITER IN WINTER

Words tickle his skull like the falling snow-
Flakes and dissolve on the pavement, his shoes
Wet and freezing his sockless feet, Olive
On his arm and Popeye pushing a pram
Through the falling snow. Olive complains of
The ever falling cold, the instruments
Frozen and still, thermostats and thermo-
Meters frozen in time. The baby cries,
The wifey—or whatever she is—whines.
Popeye the Sailor Man—*toot, toot*—trudges
Ever onward to Whole Foods for Bosc pears,
Granny Smith apples, lemons, bananas,
Cous-cous, cannellini beans, garlic, olive
Oil, and back to their overheated flat.

WILDEST DREAMS

Who could have guessed that this defeat,
This shame would be a kind of rebirth,

A second coming, and that the flaws,
The residual anger and the plummeting

Ego would herald a new person entirely,
One who cared about the smell of roses

(The feint odor of vanilla bean and lemons),
Or that this person would get to touch

You everywhere, including your thighs,
Eyelids, nose, lips, or that one might dance

Across the fog of memory with a new
Cadence, that seeing would become

A new gift, that hearing the birds in the park,
The birds, the birds, would excite such rhythms

In the air and along the roots of things
Until there was nothing but sensations,

A tinkling without the fear of, the shame for,
Being alive, the sin of being born suddenly

Become the gift of this new life you had.

MATINS

Prego, meaning, you are welcome, *si, si,*
Though originally it meant *I pray*.
I pray that you may be all right, Popeye,
Despite the adversity, Olive thought.
Prego. And I really do pray for you,
Popeye, for you. Be well and please flourish,
And to hell with the bastards who put us
Down, and it's not about them, but others,
The ones who matter to us: Swee'Pea, you.
That's who I am living for, Olive thought,
Cooking for, hanging out with, dancing with,
Loving and talking to, being among
And with, Olive told him, and he chuckled.
"And may you," Popeye said, "be ever so."

FRONTIERS

Olive's well-being's pegged to those dark woods
On the other side of that border town
At the edge of things. There is no leaving
This weight behind, as if it was a relic
Of the distant past, not an inconvenience
From recent times. Things continue to pulse
Invariably, even as she shivers
And complains bitterly about her life.
But there is no border that she comes to
Eventually, shivering and hungry,
Alone and forgotten, a refugee,
An immigrant, a migrant, a displaced
Person looking for shelter and some food.
There is no getting across this frontier.

HOW THINGS ARE THESE DAYS

There are so many hours in the day, so
Many words in my head, then comes silence,

The black hole of memory, going down
Some empty highway in a beat-up car,

Listening to the only station on
The radio, some endless right-wing talk

Show, praising the plucky billionaires and
Oligarchs in their fight against the left

And the environmentalists, and some
Old guy calls in to testify to the

Show's truth, whatever the hell he means by
Such a remark out here in the middle

Of the desert in the high heat of day,
And it all gets inside of me like a

Virus or the plague, almost like a song
You hate, but which you can't get out of your

Head all day and into the night, driving
And driving as you hum along to it.

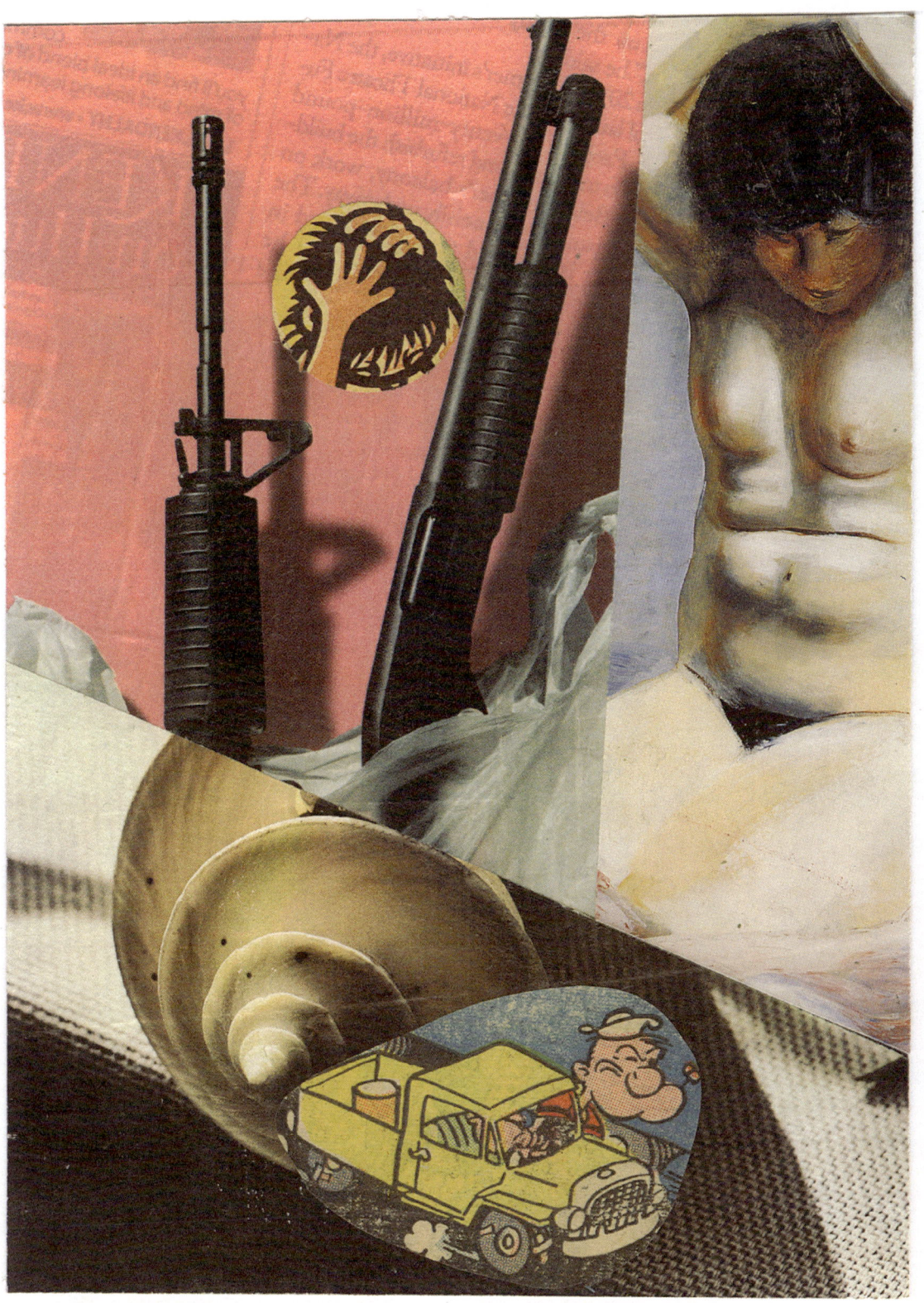

THERMALS

A kettle of hawks ride up the thermals,
Casting about for food (read here other

Birds), and just overhead, you hear that screech
Of the raptors, almost overhearing

Their conversations with each other, while
On the ground, in the bush and on the branch,

A murmuration of starlings hide, their
Heartbeats aflutter, they are afraid, their

Hush singular and collective and it,
The fear, lays across the bird colony,

Like a whisper of gossip, like talons
In the skull, the starlings hardly move in

Their hiding, silence being so great, they
Are frozen in place, like statuary.

BACCHAE

If the Bacchae come in from the spring woods,
Feed them leek and potato soup in blue

Urns with giant ladles instead of spoons,
Give them sourdough bread which melts the butter

With its white heat, the slight taste of thick salt
On their tongues, and the smell of thirst there too,

A thirst that seems unquenchable and strong,
Their urge to become domesticated

All but wiped out by the intense sunlight
And their fabricated but real passion

For this eastern god everywhere in
The lavender landscape of grapes and mint,

Thyme and oregano, bitter lemons,
Octopus and the olive oil sunsets.

SALT AIR

If you need someone to take care
Of you, I would like to offer
A hand, a heart, a broad shoulder,
And to gird my loins against all
Depredations of your salt hill
Or a fire around which a fish,
A mackerel or a bluefish,
Cooks in oil, onions, and parsley.
In the vastness of your open
Field, lean on me as wind and rain
Buffet us from patch to green patch,
The hay bales shunted off beside
The gray barn and an old tractor,
My dream is to take care of you.

EYE ON THE SPARROW

If Popeye could not concentrate, they said,
He should try to focus on one thing for
A minute, so he chose this old sparrow
That flitted from the water at his place
On the balcony, up to the old Greek's
Balcony on the fifth floor, over to
The eaves above the pub on this estate,
Then another balcony for fat balls,

Put out to stave off the winter hunger,
Along with seeds in the green bird feeder,
And back to his balcony for water
To drink and later bathe in joyously,
So that the minute did not linger like
Others said it might but flew as fast as
The sparrow, ready to live once again.

THE BLUE JAYS

When is the last time you saw a blue jay?
Long ago I saw one aggressively
Pursue the sparrows and plenty other
Birds (chickadees, nuthatches, robins, gold-
Finches in the milkweed down by the lake).
I loved the jay's blue feathers, blue as in
The sky or blue wind, though annoying as
All hell, chasing away every bird

Not a blue jay, I can't say I miss them,
And a bird that aggressive is likely
Not going to become extinct—snapping
Like that—no, the blue jay will come again
Come back to these climes one day, *am I right?*
When is the last time you saw one of them?

DIRTY LINEN

Popeye really enjoyed their company,
Though he did not always appreciate,
Women, even in groups or alone, ones
Like his mother, beautiful and also
Kind, his sisters full of energy or
Various girlfriends and partners, lovers
Or poets he met traveling across
The country and abroad, they'd talk and talk,
Mainly about books and writers or in-
Dividual poems that caught their eye,
A line that made them weep, another one
That aroused them to make love until ex-
Hausted, they lay on linen sheets, wind in
Curtains, summer's breeze opened up their hearts.

COGNITIVE DISSONANCE

It is not that Popeye forgot things, but
We all forget things. It is that he for-
Got what things were, and so he put dirty
Laundry in the refrigerator, and
Put the fish, bought that morning from the old
Fishmonger, in the laundry machine in
The basement of their building where he boxed.
He then proceeded to ask Olive what
Time were they eating dinner, not once but
Every couple of minutes, and when
It came time to ask her something else, he
Could not remember her name. Was it Jane
Or Alice or Imelda, and where was
He and what was the day, the month, or year?

HAM GRAVY

Castor Oyl commiserated with friend
Ham Gravy over being dumped by Mizz
Oyl (pronounced *Earl* as in what they put in
Cars in Brooklyn), and Castor was there to
Talk Hammy down off the ledge, his friend so
Despondent, bereft, isolated and lonely,
Alone and miserable. "That's what love
Does to a guy," Ham Gravy said, feeling
Sorry for himself in an awfully
Big way. "Olive, you have no idea,"
Ham Gravy said, "what your bony ass does
To a sorry-ass dude like me, myself
And I. Oh, Olive, I can't go on much
Longer without your lavendery scent."

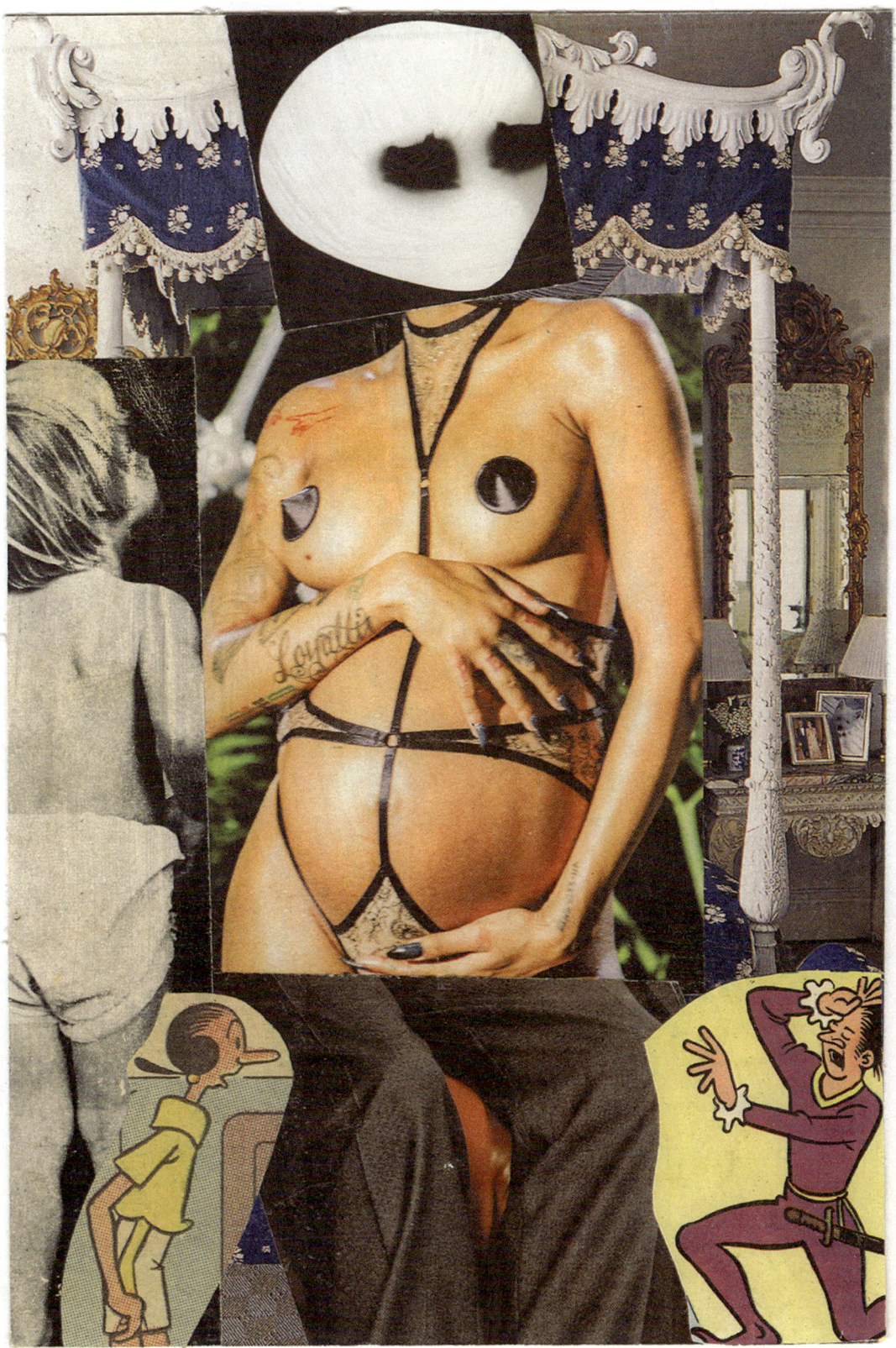

IVF

Bluto came into the bar, wearing his
Red MAGA hat, asking where Popeye was.
This evening he was angry at the
World, so why not let an embryo be
A person? Corporations were people,
Too, or so the state of Alabama
Had declared it to be so, and who was
He to dispute that fact because
It was a logic so flawless in its
Exquisite disregard, it was almost
Perfect in its tight-assed self-righteousness,
Contempt for science, something Bluto did
Not think about as he guzzled down beers,
Angry at the face he saw staring back
At him from behind the bar until he
Realized that it was his own reflection
In the bar's mirror, and he thought, why not
Let a football coach be a senator,
And why not let a corporation be
A person, let that goddamn embryo
Become a person, too, because the world
Needed more people in Alabama,
About when life began, even eggs not
Yet fertilized, as if by the fact of
Being declared that, Alabama could
Decide what life is, when it began, and
When it ended: prisoner strapped to the
Gurney for his immediate exe-
Cution, and remember: corporations
Are people, so why not embryos too?
Bluto came into the bar, wearing his
Red MAGA hat, asking where Popeye was,
So he could bash his liberal face in.
But Popeye was traveling around the
Country, getting people registered to
Vote, while Olive Oyl knocked on doors, and as
Swee'Pea stuffed envelopes for his parents,
Bluto drank an angry beer and asked some-
One near his bar stool what he was looking
At and the customer answered, "Not you,
You're too ugly," and Bluto said, "All right,"
And asked the bartender to give the man
A beer and maybe some nuts and a hard
Boiled egg or some potato chips to eat.

POPEYE AND OLIVE BECOME GEEZERS

The pyramids getting a face lift in
Giza: bullets cascade on every-
One in Gaza: supermodels pose on
The runway in a fashion show at the
Plaza, where Popeye and Olive sit front
And center, gazing at the supermod-
Els, front and center on the runway as
Time seems to crawl on with uncertainty
In Ukraine: drones attack U.S. hotspots
 In Iraq: military map of no
Certainty, uncertainty being one
Of the few things of which there is certain-
Ty, and that is that nothing is certain.
Popeye chuckles, staring at his spinach.

PRAIRIE SCHOOL

Out on the prairie, Popeye took in the
Prairie out in front of the Prairie School
House, not out on the prairie, but in town,
North of Chicago, not Frank Lloyd Wright but
Some lesser known architect, brilliant in
His own Prairie School way, the windows long
And wide, facing the wind off the great lake,
Evanston battened down for lake-effect
Snow, and several more weeks, if not months of
Winter, March wind blowing ferociously.
Olive Oyl imagined herself ensconced
In one of Evanston's Prairie School homes,
A fire in the fireplace, hot chocolate
In mugs, Bluto home from teaching Shakespeare.

PROVENDER

The real meaning of the universe is
Verse, the one verse of the world's rhythm is
Really an endless poem that is the
Story of a person's life, Popeye thought,
As he navigated his way in thick
Rush-hour traffic, as he pedaled along
On his adult tricycle, as he rode
Home, the rear basket filled with provender
For the evening's repast with Olive,
Swee'Pea, Wimpy, and even Bluto who
Brought flowers for Mizz Oyl, chocolate for
Swee'Pea, hamburgers from White Castle for
Wimpy, and even spinach for Popeye,
Though O. warned Popeye to behave or else.

SLOW FADE

He disappears, piece by piece, memory
Upon memory flushing out of him
Until he either becomes or returns
To a state that resembles tabula
Rasa; his expression each day becomes
Less expressive, blanker, empty, without
Affect or utterance, he asks her each
Couple of minutes: "What is the meeting
About?" An evaluation, she says.
"Of what?" he queries. "Your new condition,"
She tells him. "What about my condition?"
"Its progression," she says, hesitating,
"Your decline." But already he moves on
And backwards. "What is the meeting about?"

STORMY MONDAY

"They call it that," Popeye averred. "Tuesday's
Just as bad." Wimpy interrupted his
Friend, saying, "I'd gladly pay you Tuesday
For a hamburger today." Popeye laughed,
Well, he actually chortled, and stared
Into space with his one good eye, winking
At Wimpy and giving him the money,
Seventeen dollars and twelve cents, plus tax,
To buy a hamburger today, Friday,
A day where Popeye ate fish sticks, tartar
Sauce on the side with ketchup and lemons,
Worcestershire sauce because he was Cat'lic,
The Polish variety, and because
"We didn't eat meat on Friday," he said.

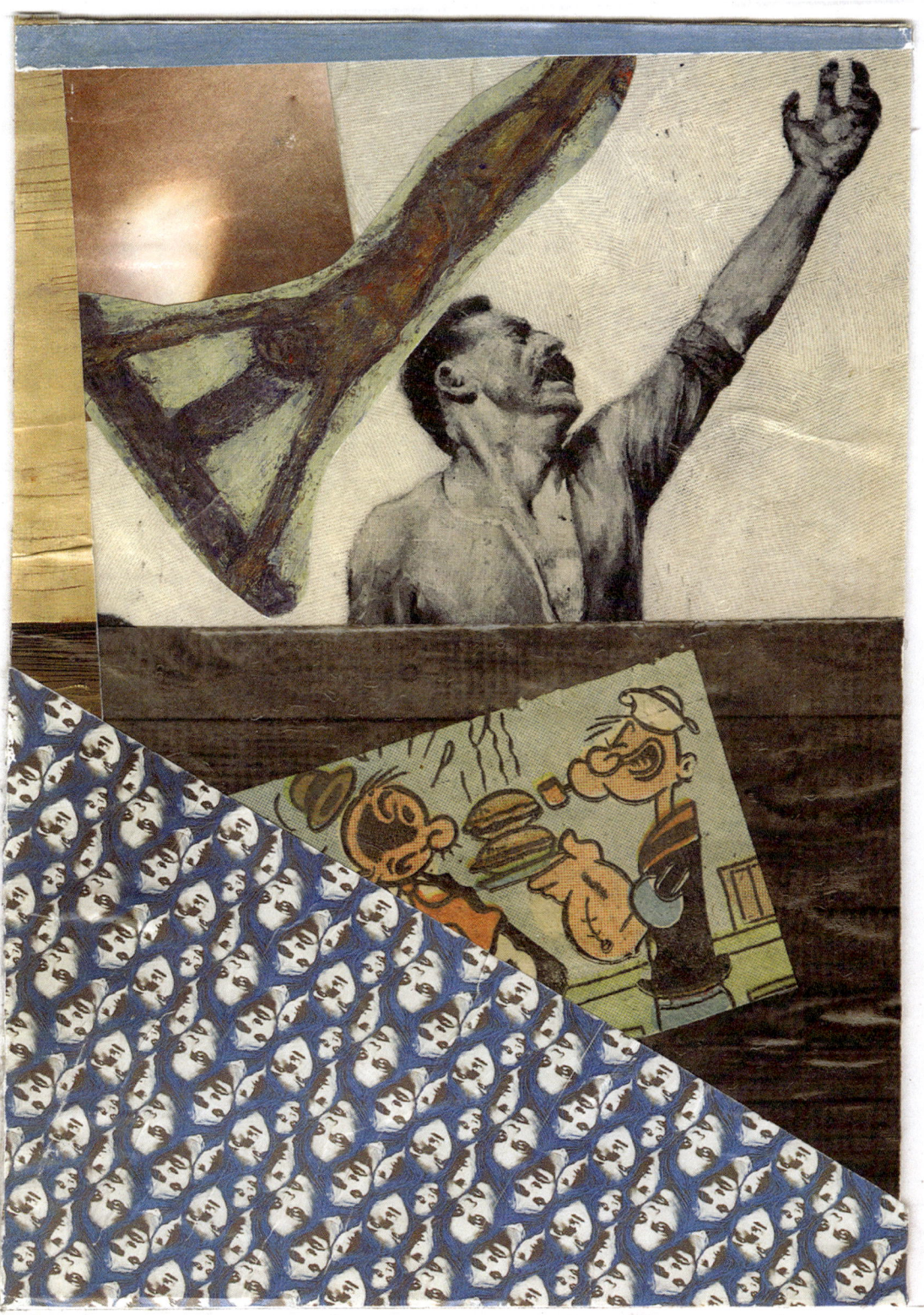

THE WAVES

Being a Sailor Man (*toot, toot*), Popeye
Had sea-legs to face any salty storm,
But like a lot of toot-tooting Sailor
Men, he did not know how to swim because,
As he once told Olive, he did not see
Any point in knowing how to swim the
Sea if his ship sunk or he fell over-
Board after all hands were called on the deck,
Only to be washed off the ship by an
Enormous rogue wave, the Sea of Japan,
Which happened to them once so many years
Ago, losing many friends and even
A few enemies, and once at Rocka-
Way pulled out and under by surging tide.

THREESOME

How did it happen, and even if a
Poem means nothing, what does this really
Mean: three men in a bed, one of them wakes,
His name Popeye, and he's sandwiched between
Wimpy on one side and Bluto on the
Other, all of them naked but for them
Wearing their undies, pee-stained and stinky.
Popeye sits up, unfurling his right hand
From Wimpy's thigh, and his left hand from the
Great Galoot's piss hard-on, Popeye thinking
That he will have some explaining to do
When he gets home to Olive Oyl's abode,
Her boudoir inviting and scented with
Lavender, patchouli, and rosemary.

FROZEN EMBRYOS

My love, my life, at night I sleep alone,
You are not here so that we can embrace
Like spoons, whispering across the night, phone
Me if you get this poem's faintest trace
Somewhere behind your benign, sweet aura,
And in that telepathy that only
Lovers have among each other or a
Prescience of where we might be, valley
Or peak, my love, my life, not wife, but love
Burning inside of each other all night
Into that time before the dawn, a glove
Fit tightly around us, please, please, hold tight,
Fasten your seat belt, my very life,
My lover, my friend, even sometime wife.

AUBADE IN SEDONA

"Is this an aubade or an alba?" asked
Popeye, as a green flash of light came at
The horizon just as Olive Oyl came
In her drawers, the sun rising up just as
Popeye came in his drawers, simultan-
Eously, in Sedona where sunrise
And sunset are almost a religious
Experience, people coming there just
To come there, sometimes sitting in lawn chairs
Outside of their campers attached to gas-
Guzzling SUVs, empty-nesters
With too much time on their hands, Popeye thought,
Holding on to Olive Oyl's shoulders as
Another wave of Sedona came on.

CARTOGRAPHY

The cartography of love is as vast
As it is certain, a map of the world,
Only internally mapped, goodness and
Grace its signposts, its own geography,
And even with its cartography, love
Has ways to elude the territory
It just defined by its scope and volume,
Even as you ask yourself, why these eyes,
Those lips, that nose, shoulders bent a certain
Way that draws you into this map's orbit,
Which you not so much acknowledge as you
Fall down its rabbit hole that was never
Mapped out by the cartographers, back in
The day: you thought you had some say in it.
You did not; you were drawn to this circle
Of light, willingly, and yet ineluct-
Ably, able and willing, full of hope.

EMINENCE STRUT

In March, we march, Popeye wrote, and we march
En masse to kick the Establishment's ass,
Up and down these lousy mean streets, full of
Rage and indignation over the wrongs
Proffered us by the rich and powerful,
From my birthday, March 4th, until the Spring,
Where the world pivots from Equinox to
Solstice, spring and summer, what's the wonder?
Though Popeye said, what isn't the wonder?
The spring's almost upon us, we sing and
Dance, we prance and strut, eminent in our
Stutter steps, moonwalking, high-stepping souls,
In love with the world's possibilities.
But don't forget injustices nearby.

GHOST OF A CHANCE

"Besides ghosting me," Olive Oyl told him—
He being Wimpy (J. Wellington him-
Self)—"God-damn Bluto gaslighted me twice,"
She went on, "telling me how much he loved
Being around me and just how interesting
I was compared to all the other gals,
All the other women he had dated
And wooed throughout the country when he played
For the Green Bay Packers as a nose-guard
On the defensive line back in the day."
"And yet, and yet, my *pamplemousse*," Wimpy
Said, "it really comes down to this, my love:
Is Popeye kosher with you performing
Various shenanigans with Bluto?"

LEGUMES

Of course there was spinach on the table,
But also salmon for its Omega-
3's, kale, walnuts, almonds, and sunflower oil,
Safflower oil, sunflower seeds, spinach,
Popeye said: "Let's not forget spinach, let's
Remember spinach's being full of
Vitamin E, an important anti-
Oxidant, and let's not forget others:
Vitamin D, great in salmon and eggs,
And, of course, Swee'Pea, there is also K,
Leafy greens where this vitamin is found."
Popeye chuckled, dreaming of citrus fruits,
Migraines and depression, which it helps to
Prevent: Magnesium. Leafy greens, nuts.

OMEGA-3

Wimpy said that it came down to fatty
Acids in Omega-3, sparking the
Brain's neurons. "They help brain cells to connect
With one another," J. Wellington slurred.
Popeye laughed and stuffed sardines into his
Gob, snorting bravely under his short breaths.
"Alpha-linolenic acid," Wimpy
Averred, "not to mention eicosapen-
Taenoic acid and, less we fail to
Recall—these neurons not sparking our thoughts—
Docosahexaenoic acid, found
In such fish as mackerel and herring,
Whose exotic smells remind this corres-
Pondent of Olive Oyl's flowing tendrils."

PARTHENOGENESIS

"Mister Popeye, have you ever heard of—
Of parthenogenesis?" Olive Oyl
Asked the one-eyed, forearmed mighty, bicep
Challenged, chortling sailor man (*toot-toot*),
Who asked his sometime lover what in God's
Broad Earth she was talking about this day,
Supposedly the first day of spring, wind
Out of the West at twenty-five miles per
Hour, as Olive told him, for instance, the
Blessed Mother was just such a virgin
Birth, and Olive observed that her giving
Birth to Swee'Pea was another instance
Of parthenogenesis, and he laughed,
Chortling into his can of spinach.

QUEL POMERIGGIO

If I leave the Atocha Station for
The falling sunlight over the Venice
Lagoon, I walk from there to Hawaii,
Sometimes, like Superman, floating, flying
Over the planet at the speed of light.
Thus I am that J. Wellington, person
Of interest, raconteur, friend of Earth,
Born and held to gravity's influence.
I saw Olive Oyl standing naked in
Front of her full-length hall mirror, admir-
Ing her subtle curves and her tensions,
She looked as good as a hamburger and
Said to me, "Don't go blabbing to Popeye
Or Bluto what we've been up to today."

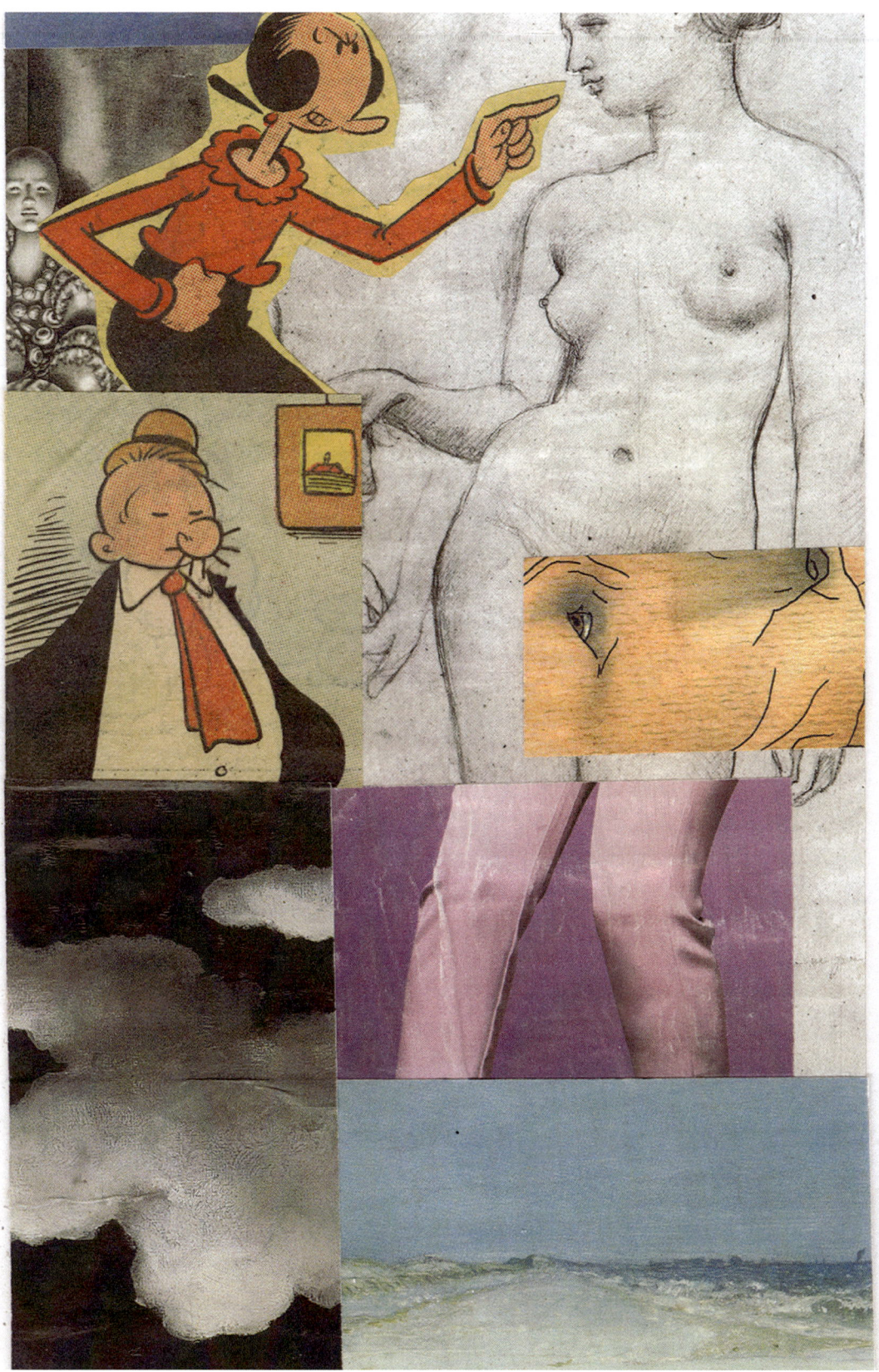

SAINT PATRICKS DAY

Wimpy wore a green plastic hat for Saint
Patrick's Day, as well as a Six Nation's
Rugby football shirt with shamrocks on the
Green cloth, a bit tipsy was J. Welling-
Ton as he attempted to navigate
Stephens Green on his way to a party
At the American ambassador
To Ireland's residence, jackassery
Everywhere about the street in snot
Green Dublin on this Saint's holy day of
Of no obligation, the Liffey full
Of green puke by American hordes of
Invaders who traced their Irishness back
To grand Potato Famine ancestors.

SAPPHIC ALBA

In the moonlight Olive Oyl's curls are like
Tendrils, holding Peaches Avocado's
Hand. "Girls will be girls," she said, as they groped
Each other, and the moonlit sky turned to
Dawn out on the prairie where the two got
To know each other intimately with
Deep tongue kisses, sparking a new romance—
A new idea for romance—as they
Went at it in the back of Peaches' truck,
The country music in the cool night air,
And each declaring her undying love
For the other, although the next day, back
With her sometime beau Popeye, she said to
Herself, "Now, girl, what was that all about?"

SPRING RINGS ROUND

Conglomerations of cherry tree leaves
Leave the branch and float down to Earth, forming
A petal-bed at Olive Oyl's feet (size
9, by the way), and she runs among them,
Kicking up a profusion of pink and
White flowers, still alive after leaving
The prospect of trees near the Central Park
Reservoir, screaming, "Oh, Popeye, they are
So beautiful." Just then Popeye, out of
The corner of his one good eye (good day,
Mate), he spots Jacqueline Kennedy O-
Nassis, surrounded by Secret Service
Joggers, wearing a Versace colored
Scarf on her head, she says hello, goodbye,
As she jogs off around the Reservoir.

TARGET

"What's the point?" Olive asked, the
Point being this word "point" forming
Like a decaying tooth end of
The word *price*. "Is it needed or
Can we jettison it simply
For the word *price*?" But just then Pope-
Eye came home from work down the piers,
Declaring that "the price point was
All fucked up down at the super-
Market," where he had been shopping
For eggs, smoked salmon, lemons and
Er, bunches of fresh spinach which
He planned to use with the blender
He bought yesterday at Target.

THE BIG GUY

"Language is my ax," Bluto averred in
The Brooklyn loft of Olive Oyl, and she,
Being suddenly coquettish, batted
Her kohl-farded eyes, and whispered to him,
"Eat your éclair, Big Guy, and let's be real
With each other. I want you so bad, it
Makes me ache all over, I'm wet, I'm hard,
I'm happy, I'm horny, I'm aroused, I'm
Ready for you in the bedroom, Galoot."
But Bluto was sitting in the La-Z-
Boy chair in the living room corner, eyes
Half-lidded and blank, staring at the blank
Screen on the TV set, center-stage, he
Blubberingly snored, steadily, loudly.

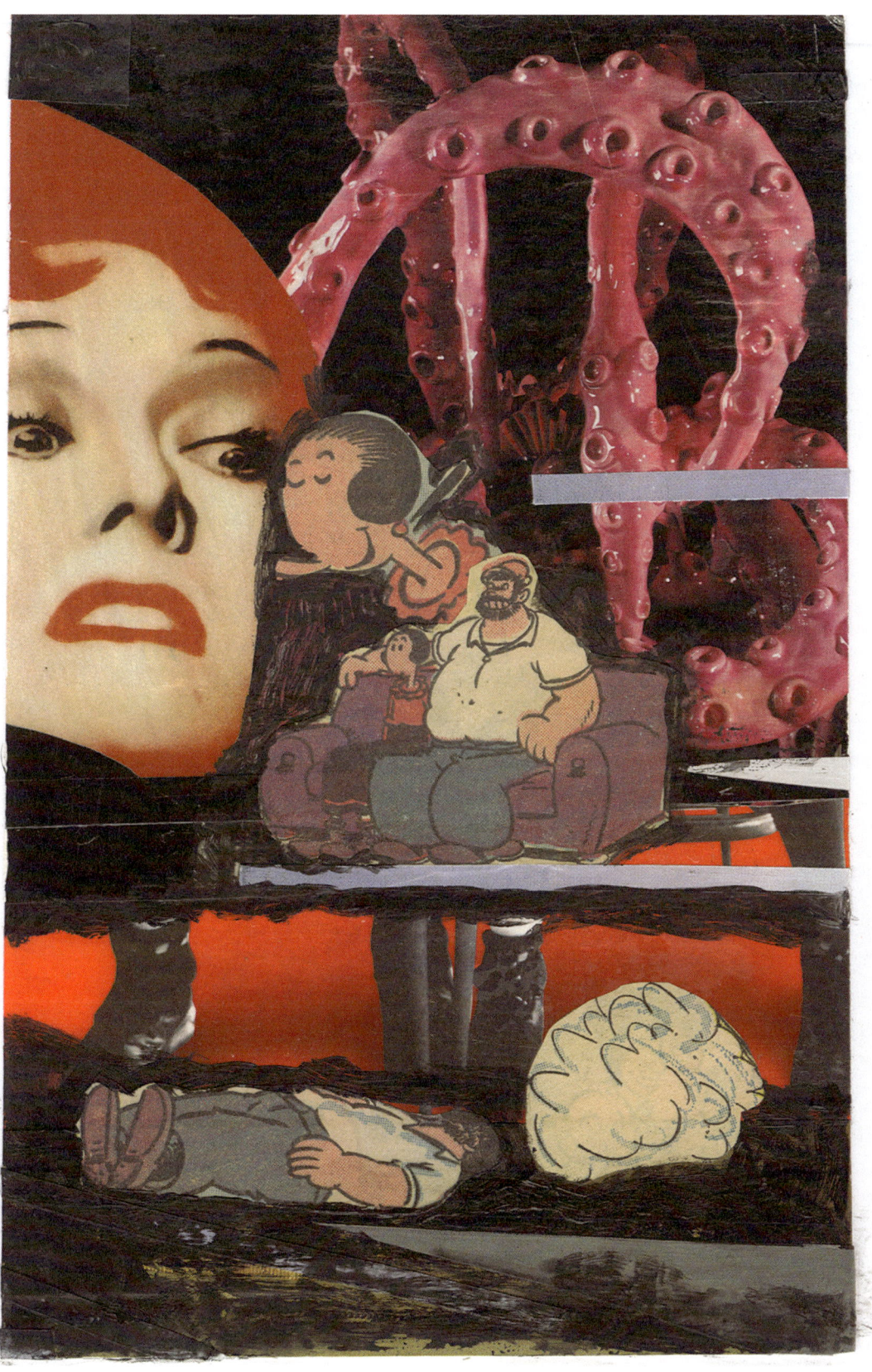

WIMPY'S DREAM

She turned to me and looked as good as a
Hamburger, which I would gladly pay her
Tuesday to have at it today, today
Being Wednesday, a day which reminds me
Of Wensleydale cheese, something that Wallace
And Gromit ate regularly, bringing
Out their refreshing smiles, which I miss now-
Adays, and the days they seem to roll past
Like horses in the dust of the prairie,
Which reminds me further of that woman
Who in turn reminded of hamburger,
One topped up with lettuce and tomato,
Raw onion, mustard, relish, ketchup, and
Other condiments as is my wanton-
Ness, as is my way of life, tramp I am.

BUDDY BOLDEN'S BOUNCE

(September 6, 1877- November 4, 1931)

Having invented jazz, Buddy Bolden
Tried to imagine what else he'd invent,

Maybe the light bulb or dry cereal,
A cure for syphilis or dementia

Praecox, something he was familiar
With, but he stuck with jazz, American

And quintessential as coffee with milk
And sugar, shrimp gumbo or chicory,

The scent of magnolia blossoms fallen
To the ground after rain. The smell of earth

After rain, cornet in hand, he climbed up
A funky tree in New Orleans, played us

We-the-people music, then flew away
From that perch, never to be seen again.

DEAD POETS

With Popeye and Olive Oyl, the Sea Hag
Held a séance at her Bed-Stuy Brooklyn
Brownstone, sitting them in the late after-
Noon parlour with some Trader Joe's ginger
Cookies and some Irish afternoon tea.
Popeye thought about his own early days
In this borough, drinking in Tromer's beer
Garden, and getting in bar fights with some
Strangers from far away County Mayo,
When the Sea Hag said she was getting strong
Signals from the beyond. "Possibly was
It Frank O'Hara?" Popeye asked the Hag
Who said: "Does the name Elio Schneeman
Ring a bell with any of youse people?"

THE MIGRATION OF BIRDS

I am in love with the day because of
The clear light or the blue sky and your eyes
Or I am in love with the white clouds and
The muted colors of the leaves on the
Trees and the migration of birds in air
And on the ground and in the trees and dogs
Barking or dogs running about or just there or
This park bench off to the side away from
Everyone this pond full of ducks and coots
The imperious swans and the humble
Geese and even the majestic herons
And I love the smell in the air and chill
Behind the sunlight and I love this bench
Where we once sat talking about such things

LIKE SISYPHUS, POPEYE PUSHED A ROCK

Like Sisyphus, Popeye pushed a rock up
A steep incline, and each time he got near
The top, he plummeted backwards into
A pit far below, a region without
Light or air, a nether world, from which he
Emerged, rolling the rock upwards again,
Earlier he had eaten spinach, and
Powered forward into the incline, he
Pushed the rock up and onwards, and halfway,
A woman in new Nike running shoes
And pink athleisurewear, she waved hello
To Popeye, and he nodded back to her.
She pushed an expensive baby buggy,
And said to him: "Loser buys the lattes."

M. G. STEPHENS is author of over 30 books, most recently *Popeye, Unchained*, poetry and collages, a collaboration with Brooklyn artist Archie Rand; and *Come On, Eileen*, fiction. In 2022, Spuyten Duyvil published two Stephens novels, *King Ezra*, about Modernist poet Ezra Pound; and *Kid Coole*, the third book in the Coole cycle of novels, the other books being *Season at Coole* and *The Brooklyn Book of the Dead*. Paycock Press published a collection of Stephens' stories, *Jesus' Dog* in 2024.

ARCHIE RAND is an artist whose six-decade career has produced stained glass, murals, illustrations and over 100 solo exhibitions. His paintings and graphic works are in major museums and collections worldwide. Frequently collaborating with poets and texts, he is the author of the best-selling book, *The 613* (Penguin/Random House, 2015). Awarded numerous honors he is a Guggenheim Fellow and had served as Chair of the Columbia University Department of Visual Arts. He is currently the CUNY Presidential Professor of Art at Brooklyn College. Recent published works include *Blood Moon* with Anne Waldman (Freight & Volume, 2022), *Single Occupancy* with Lewis Warsh (Cuneiform Press, 2023), *The Seventeen: Iron Flock* (HUC/Skirball Museum, 2024) and *Popeye, Unchained* with M.G. Stephens (Spuyten Duyvil, 2025).

www.ingramcontent.com/pod-product-compliance
Lightning Source LLC
Chambersburg PA
CBRC090832120626
46547CB00009B/665